ALIEN
by Dan

Illustrated by
Aleksandar Sotirovski

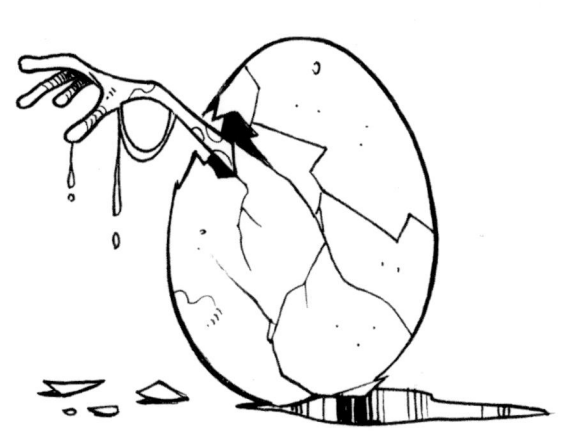

Titles in More First Flight

Comic Chaos	Jonny Zucker
Into The Deep	Jonny Zucker
Cyber Phone	Richard Taylor
Mutt	Jane A C West
Captured!	Alison Hawes
Robot Goalie	Roger Hurn
Alien Eggs	Danny Pearson
Just in Time	Jane A C West
The Speed Flyers	Jonny Zucker
Super Teacher	Stan Cullimore

Badger Publishing Limited
Oldmedow Road, Hardwick Industrial Estate,
King's Lynn PE30 4JJ
Telephone: 01438 791037

www.badgerlearning.co.uk

2 4 6 8 10 9 7 5 3 1

Alien Eggs ISBN 978 1 84926 460 0

First edition © 2011
Second edition © 2015

Text © Danny Pearson 2011
Complete work © Badger Publishing Limited 2011

All rights reserved. No part of this publication may be reproduced, stored in any form or by any means mechanical, electronic, recording or otherwise without the prior permission of the publisher.

The right of Danny Pearson to be identified as author of this Work has been asserted by him in accordance with the Copyright, Designs and Patents Act 1988.

Badger Publishing would like to thank Jonny Zucker for his help in putting this series together.

Publisher: David Jamieson
Senior Editor: Danny Pearson
Design: Fiona Grant
Illustration: Aleksandar Sotirovski

Alien Eggs

Contents

Chapter 1	**Fright Night**	page 5
Chapter 2	**Breakfast**	page 10
Chapter 3	**Food Fight**	page 14
Chapter 4	**The Barn**	page 19
Chapter 5	**Goodbye Gifts**	page 23
Mysteries		page 30
Questions		page 32

New words:

barn	froze
creatures	spaceship
alien	skinny

Main characters:

Laura

Ruth

Josh

Chapter 1
Fright Night

Ruth and Laura were getting ready to watch 'Alien Invaders'.

Ruth was Laura's best friend and they were having a sleepover.

"I can't wait to get this film started. I have been waiting ages to watch this," said Laura.

"Yeah, I have heard it is really scary," Ruth replied.

They put on the film and began to watch it.

The film was very scary and both girls were watching it from behind their pillows.

The main hero of the film was in a dark room. He could hear a strange sound coming from behind a door. He reached out to open the door when…

"ARGHHHHHH!" Ruth and Laura screamed.

Laura's little brother had come bursting through the bedroom door just as one of the aliens jumped out of the shadows in the film.

"Get out, get out!" Laura screamed. "Mum! Josh is in my room again!"

"Josh, get out of your sister's room and leave them to watch their film in peace," Laura's mum shouted.

Laura chased Josh down the stairs, hitting him with her pillow.

Ruth paused the film and waited for her to get back.

Suddenly a flash of light came from outside the bedroom window.

"What was that?" Ruth whispered.

She walked over to the window.
She could see light coming from the barn.
"Laura!" Ruth shouted.

"What's up with you?" asked Laura. "You look like you have seen a ghost."

"I think I have, I just saw light coming from your barn."

"Yes, of course you did," Laura replied with a smile. "I think the film has got you a little bit scared, maybe it is time for bed."

"Maybe you are right, maybe it was just my imagination," Ruth smiled.

Chapter 2
Breakfast

Ruth and Laura woke up early and headed down for breakfast.

Josh was already at the table.

"Good morning, girls. Did the aliens get you?" Josh laughed.

"Shut up you!" they both said at the same time.

"Where are mum and dad?" asked Laura.

"Oh they have already gone out to work on the farm. They needed to make an early start," Josh replied. "They said that you should cook my breakfast."

Now Josh had a huge smile on his face. "Come on, get to it," he snapped.

Laura was not happy about this, but she was hungry so she started to get breakfast ready.

"Sit down Ruth, I'll make a start on breakfast."

"Mmmmm eggs, you are so lucky to live on a farm, your food is so fresh," said Ruth.

Just then one egg from the basket in the middle of the table began to move.

"Erm Laura, I think your eggs may be a little too fresh... one seems to be moving."

"What?" Laura asked as she walked over to the table.

All three of them leaned over to the basket of eggs.

Again one of the eggs moved.
Then cracked.

Josh was so excited. "Yes, my very own baby chick!"

The egg cracked again and a long, skinny grey arm appeared.

"Josh, that is no chick!" Ruth said with terror in her voice.

Chapter 3
Food Fight

The grey skinny arm began to break the egg shell and suddenly a small creature popped out.

Ruth and Laura jumped back away from the table leaving Josh standing there.

"Cool! This is way better than a chick."

"Get away from the table Josh, you don't know what it wants," said Laura.

"It's an alien! They have come to take over the planet. We are all doomed!" screamed Ruth.

"Calm down," said Laura. "It is not an alien and we are not doomed. Look at the size of it, and there is only one of him and three of us."

Just then the other eggs started to move.

"Yes, more of them!" shouted Josh.

One by one the eggs started to break open to reveal more little creatures.

"Josh, get back now!" both girls demanded.

"No, they are mine. Look they are friendly, maybe they are hungry," Josh said softly.

He handed one of the creatures a piece of toast.

The creature had big friendly eyes and a tiny smile on its face as it made its way over to Josh and his toast.

In a flash the creature's smile had gone and it jumped for the toast, ripping it from Josh's hands.

"OK, I don't want them any more," Josh declared as he backed away from the table.

The other creatures started to fight over the food that was on the table, and after that had gone they began to raid the kitchen cupboards.

"Let's get out of here!" all the kids shouted.

Chapter 4
The Barn

The three of them ran outside and locked the door behind them.

"What on Earth is going on?" asked Laura.

"I don't think those creatures are from Earth," answered Ruth. "Where did those eggs come from?"

Josh pointed to the barn. It was then that they noticed the barn was moving and they could hear the hens inside making loud noises.

Laura ran over to the barn doors.

"The eggs, there are more inside the barn – we have to help the hens. OK, on the count of three, Josh you open up the doors," Laura ordered.

"No way, I don't want to get eaten," he said.

Ruth pushed Josh to one side. "I'll do it. OK, on three... one... two...THREE!"

Laura opened the barn doors and the hens burst out.

"OK, that's all of them – quick, shut the doors!" Josh screamed.

He could see a whole group of tiny creatures eating all the hen food.

The creatures looked up and started running towards the open doors.

"QUICKLY!" Josh screamed again.

Laura and Ruth managed to shut the doors just in time.

They heard a loud thud and then scratching sounds against the doors as the creatures tried to break them down.

Laura backed away from the barn, "OK I think we are safe."

Just as she said that the creatures from inside the house smashed the kitchen window and began to pour out of it.

"Oh no we are not," sighed Josh.

Chapter 5
Goodbye Gifts

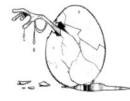

The little creatures ran straight towards them.

"They are going to eat us!" Ruth cried.

But the creatures ran straight past them and to the barn doors.

They climbed onto each other's shoulders and the top one opened the doors to let the others out.

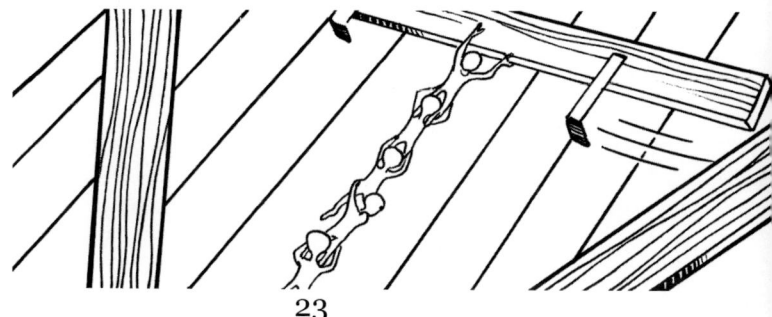

They all grouped together, then ran straight towards the nearby cornfield.

"What are they doing? What is going on?" asked Ruth.

"Looks like they are hungry, it is breakfast time after all," answered Josh.

The three of them watched on as the field was being stripped of corn.

Then a giant spaceship appeared
from the sky.

Josh couldn't take any more of this.
"Oh this is perfect, they are aliens, and
now there are more of them, we are in
big trouble."

The alien creatures froze and watched
the ship land in front of the barn.

A loud sound like a giant horn came
from the ship, and a ramp appeared
from the side.

The alien creatures lined up in a straight line and started to walk calmly up the ramp onto the ship.

Two larger aliens appeared and walked down the ramp and over to them.

"They are going to eat our brains!" Ruth shrieked.

"Excuse me, we are not going to eat your brains," one of the aliens said with a friendly smile on its face.

"We are ever so sorry about this, we usually make it back in time before they hatch. You see, the best way to grow our young is in what you call hen eggs."

"That's the only way you can grow your young?" asked Josh.

"No, it is not the only way," replied the alien. "But it is the best way. We do this every few thousand of your Earth years."

"Again, we are sorry. We shall leave you a few gifts. It is the least we can do."

"Erm OK, thanks, I guess," said Laura.

And with that the aliens went back to their spaceship and started to take off.

The ship hung in the air for a while, then a beam shot out.

Ruth, Laura and Josh couldn't believe what had appeared in front of them.

"WOW! My very own wonders of the world."

Mysteries

Stonehenge
Stonehenge could have been built to watch the Sun's or the Moon's movements. However, some believe that aliens were involved with the building of Stonehenge. It could have been built to worship the aliens.

Easter Island statues
Easter Island is one of the most remote islands on Earth. On the island there are statues shaped like eyeless faces.

The biggest one, Paro, weighs about 82 tonnes and measures over 9 metres.,

No one knows how and why they were built.

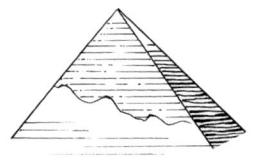

Pyramids

Some people believe that the pyramids found in Egypt were built by aliens.

A few of the pyramids even line up exactly with the stars in the night sky.

Strange images of alien-type creatures appear on the inside walls of pyramids.

Egyptian writing tells about the sky opening and lights shining down on them.

Could these lights have been alien spaceships?

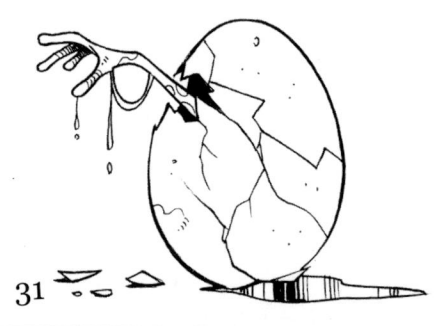

Questions

- *What film were Ruth and Laura watching?*

- *What did Josh give the first creature to eat?*

- *How many large aliens appeared from the spaceship?*

- *What gifts did the aliens leave Laura, Ruth and Josh?*

- *If aliens did visit Earth, what do you think they would look like?*